THE STORY

OF

ST. BRIDGET

A JOURNEY OF FAITH AND TRANSFORMATION OF ST. BRIDGET OF SWEDEN

D0089510

Table of Contents

Introduction

St. Bridget, also known as Bridget of Sweden or Birgitta of Sweden was a remarkable figure whose life and legacy continue to inspire people around the world. Born in the fourteenth century, she emerged as a prominent mystic, religious leader, and founder of the Bridgettine Order. Her profound spiritual experiences, influential writings and interactions with kings and popes shaped the course of her life and left an indelible mark on the religious landscape of medieval Europe.

This book seeks to delve into the life and journey of St. Bridget, exploring the rich tapestry of her experiences, teachings, and impact on society. Through a captivating narrative, we will trace her footsteps from her humble beginnings to her significant role in medieval spirituality.

To understand St. Bridget's life, it is essential to consider the historical context in which she lived. The fourteenth century was a time of great religious fervor, political upheaval, and societal transformation. Europe was grappling with the aftermath of the Black Death, a devastating pandemic that claimed countless lives. It was a period marked by religious schisms with the Papal Schism dividing the Church and eroding its authority. In the midst of these tumultuous times, St. Bridget emerged as a beacon of faith and a voice of spiritual renewal.

In the first chapter, we will explore St. Bridget's early life and background. Born into a devout family, she experienced a formative upbringing that laid the foundation for her later spiritual journey. We will delve into her childhood, examining the influences that shaped her beliefs and values. As she grew older, St. Bridget's deepening connection with God set her on a path of profound devotion and contemplation.

Chapter two focuses on a pivotal turning point in St. Bridget's life—a transformative spiritual awakening. It was during this period that she began to receive vivid visions and divine revelations. These mystical experiences ignited a burning passion within her to serve God and seek a higher purpose. We will delve into the significance of these revelations and the ways in which they shaped St. Bridget's subsequent actions and teachings.

The subsequent chapter will explore St. Bridget's role as a trailblazer and the founder of the Bridgettine Order. We will delve into the challenges she faced in establishing the first convent and the subsequent expansion of her religious community. The chapter will shed light on the unique teachings and practices of the Bridgettine Order, as well as their enduring impact on the spiritual landscape of medieval Europe.

St. Bridget's spiritual insights and writings constitute a significant aspect of her legacy, which will be explored in chapter four. Her written works, including revelations, prayers, and spiritual guidance, were influential during her time and continue to resonate with readers today. We will examine the key themes in her writings and the ways in which they offered solace, guidance, and inspiration to her contemporaries.

Chapter five will take us on a journey alongside St. Bridget as she embarked on pilgrimages and travels. These journeys allowed her to connect with other spiritual leaders, gain insights from diverse cultures, and deepen her understanding of God's creation. We will delve into the impact of these experiences on her spiritual journey and the lessons she learned along the way.

St. Bridget's interactions with kings and popes will be the focus of chapter six. Her unique position as a revered spiritual figure granted her access to influential leaders, enabling her to advocate for social justice and religious reforms. We will explore the relationships she formed with royalty, her influence on political and religious decision-making, and her commitment to addressing the pressing issues of her time.

The book concludes by examining St. Bridget's lasting legacy and her ongoing relevance in the modern world. We will reflect on the lessons to be learned from her life and example, as well as the ways in which her teachings continue to inspire individuals seeking spiritual guidance and meaning.

Through this exploration of St. Bridget's life and legacy, we hope to shed light on her remarkable journey and the profound impact she had on the religious and social landscape of medieval Europe. Join us on this captivating journey as we unravel "The Story of St. Bridget" and discover the timeless wisdom and inspiration she imparts to us today.

The significance of St. Bridget

The significance of St. Bridget, also known as Bridget of Sweden or Birgitta of Sweden, lies in her profound impact on the religious, social, and cultural spheres of medieval Europe. Her life and teachings continue to resonate with people today, making her a figure of enduring significance. Here are some key aspects that highlight the significance of St. Bridget:

1. Mystical Spirituality: St. Bridget's profound mystical experiences, including visions and divine revelations, positioned her as a significant mystic of her time. Her spiritual encounters and insights offered a unique perspective on the divine, inspiring others to deepen their own spiritual connections and seek a closer relationship with God.

2. Founder of the Bridgettine Order: St. Bridget's establishment of the Bridgettine Order, also known as the Order of the Most Holy Savior, showcased her visionary leadership. This religious community, combining elements of monasticism and active ministry, played a crucial role in

fostering spiritual growth, education, and charitable works. The Bridgettine Order became renowned for its dedication to prayer, scholarship, and social service, leaving a lasting impact on medieval religious life.

3. Spiritual Guidance and Writings: St. Bridget's writings, primarily her Revelations, Prayers, and Exhortations, hold great significance. Her works offered spiritual guidance, practical advice, and reflections on various aspects of faith, morality, and devotion. These writings not only influenced her contemporaries but continue to inspire and provide insights into the spiritual life for readers across generations.

4. Interactions with Royalty and Church Leaders: St. Bridget's close relationships with kings, queens, and influential church leaders elevated her voice and allowed her to advocate for social justice, reforms, and religious unity. She fearlessly addressed issues such as corruption, moral decay, and political strife, using her influence to encourage positive change and promote a deeper commitment to Christian values.

5. Canonization and Veneration: St. Bridget's canonization by Pope Boniface IX in 1391 elevated her to the status of a saint within the Catholic Church. Her formal recognition as a holy figure demonstrated the widespread recognition of her sanctity and the significance of her life's work. St. Bridget's feast day on July 23rd continues to be celebrated by the faithful, and her relics and shrines attract pilgrims from around the world.

5. Historical and Cultural Influence: St. Bridget's impact extended beyond her immediate time and place. Her life and teachings shaped the religious landscape of medieval Europe, offering a model of faith, piety, and devotion. The Bridgettine Order's expansion across different countries further disseminated her ideals and practices. Additionally, St. Bridget's legacy inspired later spiritual figures and writers, contributing to the broader tapestry of Christian mysticism and spirituality.

The significance of St. Bridget lies in her mystical experiences, the establishment of the Bridgettine Order, her influential writings, and her interactions with royalty and church leaders. Her canonization and ongoing veneration, as well as her historical and cultural impact, further highlight the enduring significance of her life and teachings. St. Bridget's profound spirituality and commitment to social reform continue to inspire individuals seeking spiritual growth and a deeper connection with God.

Historical context and background

To understand the historical context and background of St. Bridget's life, it is important to delve into the fourteenth century, the era in which she lived. This period was marked by significant historical, religious, and social changes that shaped the world in which St. Bridget emerged as a prominent figure.

The fourteenth century witnessed a Europe recovering from the devastating impact of the Black Death. The bubonic plague, which ravaged the continent in the mid-1300s, resulted in widespread death and social upheaval. The loss of millions of lives had profound effects on the social economic, and religious structures of the time. The trauma and fear caused by the plague prompted a deepened focus on mortality, spiritual reflection and religious devotion.

Additionally, the fourteenth century was a time of political and religious turbulence. The Papal Schism, which began in 1378, divided the Catholic Church into factions supporting rival popes, each claiming legitimacy. This schism eroded the authority of the Church and fueled confusion and discord among the faithful.

Amidst these challenging circumstances, St. Bridget was born in Sweden in 1303. Sweden itself was undergoing significant changes during that period The country was transitioning from a decentralized feudal society to a more centralized monarchy. It was also experiencing the effects of the Teutonic Knights' presence, who played a significant role in the political and religious landscape of the region.

St. Bridget came from a devout family, and her upbringing provided a strong foundation for her spiritual journey. She received an education befitting her social status, which was unusual for women of that time. Her marriage to

Ulf Gudmarsson, a nobleman, further connected her to the influential circles of Swedish society.

During her early years, St. Bridget experienced visions and divine revelations that shaped her spirituality. These mystical experiences fueled her devotion to God and prompted her to dedicate her life to serving Him. Her commitment to her faith led her to establish the Bridgettine Order, which combined elements of monasticism and active ministry, emphasizing prayer, study, and works of charity.

St. Bridget's influence extended beyond Sweden. She embarked on pilgrimages to Rome and the Holy Land, encountering prominent religious figures and political leaders along the way. These encounters further solidified her position as a respected spiritual leader, and her counsel was sought by kings, queens, and even popes.

St. Bridget's role as an advisor to royalty and her writings advocating for moral and social reform exemplify her engagement with the political and religious affairs of her time. She fearlessly addressed corruption, moral decay, and the need for unity within the Catholic Church.

Ultimately, St. Bridget's life unfolded within a complex historical context characterized by the aftermath of the Black Death, the Papal Schism, political transformations in Sweden, and the influence of the Teutonic Knights. Her spiritual experiences, leadership, and interactions with influential figures allowed her to make a significant impact on the religious and social landscape of medieval Europe. St. Bridget's teachings and legacy continue to inspire individuals seeking spiritual guidance, making her a figure of enduring historical and cultural significance.

Chapter One

Early Life and Background

1.1 Birth and family of St. Bridget

St. Bridget, also known as Bridget of Sweden or Birgitta of Sweden, was born around the year 1303 in the town of Finsta in Uppland, Sweden. She was born into a noble and devout Christian family, which played a significant role in shaping her early life and spiritual upbringing.

Her father, Birger Persson, was a wealthy landowner and governor of the province of Uppland. He held a prominent position in Swedish society and had close connections with the royal court. St. Bridget's mother, Ingeborg Bengtsdotter, also came from a noble lineage, and her family had ties to the Swedish aristocracy.

St. Bridget's family was deeply religious, and they instilled in her a strong faith and a commitment to Christian values from an early age. She grew up surrounded by the teachings of the Church, and her parents emphasized the importance of prayer, piety, and charitable acts.

In her youth, St. Bridget received an education befitting her noble status, which was relatively uncommon for girls during that time. She learned to read and write, studying both secular and religious texts. This education played a crucial role in shaping her later life as a writer and religious leader.

When St. Bridget was around thirteen years old, her parents arranged her marriage to Ulf Gudmarsson, a nobleman from the prominent Ulvåsa family. The marriage was politically motivated, cementing alliances between influential families. Together, St. Bridget and Ulf had eight children, four sons, and four daughters.

Despite her marital responsibilities, St. Bridget remained deeply committed to her faith and sought to live a life dedicated to God. Her marriage was characterized by mutual respect and support, with Ulf supporting St. Bridget's spiritual endeavors. They embarked on pilgrimages together, and Ulf was known to be a pious and devout husband.

After approximately twenty years of marriage, Ulf passed away in 1344. This event marked a significant turning point in St. Bridget's life. She levoted herself even more fervently to her spiritual pursuits and embraced a life of asceticism and prayer.

Following her husband's death, St. Bridget experienced a series of mystical visions and revelations, which deepened her commitment to God and her desire to serve Him. These experiences shaped her spiritual journey and inspired her to found the Bridgettine Order, a religious community dedicated to prayer, study, and works of charity.

St. Bridget's family played a supportive role in her religious vocation. Her children, including her daughter Catherine, actively participated in the work of the Bridgettine Order and supported their mother's endeavors.

The birth and upbringing of St. Bridget within a noble and devout family contributed to the strong foundation of faith that guided her throughout her life. Her family's influence, combined with her own spiritual experiences, led her to become a revered figure in Christian history, inspiring countless individuals through her teachings, writings, and example of dedicated service to God.

1.2 Childhood and upbringing

St. Bridget, also known as Bridget of Sweden or Birgitta of Sweden, had a childhood and upbringing that played a significant role in shaping her spiritual journey and eventual vocation as a religious leader. Born in th early 14th century, her early years were marked by the influence of he devout Christian family and the cultural and religious milieu of medieva Sweden.

Bridget was born into a noble family in the town of Finsta in Uppland Sweden, around the year 1303. Her father, Birger Persson, held a positio of influence as a wealthy landowner and the governor of the province o Uppland. Her mother, Ingeborg Bengtsdotter, also came from a nobl lineage with connections to the Swedish aristocracy. Bridget grew up in a environment of privilege and relative social prominence.

From an early age, Bridget was exposed to the teachings and practices o the Catholic Church. Her family instilled in her a deep sense of faith and commitment to Christian values. Bridget's parents played a crucial role i nurturing her spiritual development and fostering a strong religiou foundation.

Bridget received an education that was uncommon for girls during that time She learned to read and write, studying both secular and religious texts. Thi education provided her with the tools to engage with intellectual an spiritual pursuits later in life.

As a child, Bridget would have attended religious services regularly, participating in Mass and engaging in prayers and devotions. The liturgical calendar and the rhythms of the Church would have shaped her understanding of the Christian faith and its various feast days and traditions.

Bridget's upbringing also exposed her to the broader cultural and religious influences of medieval Sweden. The country was undergoing significant social and political changes during her childhood, transitioning from a decentralized feudal society to a more centralized monarchy. The influence of the Catholic Church in Sweden was growing, and religious practices and traditions permeated daily life.

It is likely that Bridget's family had connections with local clergy and religious communities, further exposing her to the spiritual and religious discourse of the time. These influences, along with her personal experiences and encounters, would lay the groundwork for her later spiritual awakening and vocation as a mystic and religious leader.

The values of piety, prayer, and devotion that Bridget learned in her childhood would remain central to her throughout her life. They formed the bedrock of her spirituality and guided her actions and beliefs as she embarked on a remarkable journey of religious service and reform.

Bridget's upbringing within a devout Christian family and her exposure to the religious and cultural influences of medieval Sweden shaped her worldview and prepared her for the profound spiritual experiences and leadership role that awaited her in adulthood. Her childhood experiences, combined with her own personal devotion and spiritual encounters, would ultimately propel her to become one of the most influential figures in the religious landscape of medieval Europe.

1.3 Influences and religious experiences

St. Bridget of Sweden was deeply influenced by various factors and religious experiences throughout her life. These influences played a crucial role in shaping her spiritual journey and the development of her unique religious perspective. Here are some of the key influences and religious experiences that impacted St. Bridget:

1. Family and Upbringing: St. Bridget's upbringing within a devout Christian family laid the foundation for her faith. Her parents instilled in her a strong commitment to Christian values, and her family environment fostered an atmosphere of piety, prayer, and devotion. The influence of her family provided her with a solid spiritual foundation that would guide her throughout her life.

2. Early Devotional Practices: As a young girl, St. Bridget participated in regular religious practices and devotions. She attended Mass, engaged in prayers, and immersed herself in the liturgical calendar and traditions of the Catholic Church. These early devotional practices cultivated her love for God and shaped her understanding of the Christian faith.

3. Mystical Experiences and Visions: St. Bridget's spiritual journey was marked by numerous mystical experiences and visions. From the age of seven, she claimed to receive divine revelations and vivid visions that provided her with insights into the spiritual realm. These experiences deepened her sense of connection with God and fueled her commitment to a life of prayer and devotion.

4. Personal Prayer and Contemplation: St. Bridget dedicated significant time to personal prayer and contemplation. She sought solitude and silence to commune with God, engaging in deep reflection and spiritual exercises. Through these practices, she developed a profound sense of intimacy with the divine and an acute awareness of God's presence in her life.

5. Pilgrimages and Sacred Sites: St. Bridget embarked on several pilgrimages to holy sites, including Rome and Jerusalem. These journeys allowed her to immerse herself in the rich spiritual history and traditions associated with these sacred places. The experiences she encountered

during these pilgrimages deepened her spirituality and provided her with a broader perspective on the universal nature of the Church.

6. Spiritual Directors and Advisors: St. Bridget sought guidance from trusted spiritual directors and advisors throughout her life. These individuals played a significant role in shaping her spiritual journey, offering insights, support, and counsel. Notably, the Dominican theologian, Peter Olivi, and her confessor, Master Matthias, provided her with invaluable guidance and support.

7. Religious Texts and Scripture: St. Bridget had a deep reverence for sacred texts, including the Bible and religious writings of the time. She immersed herself in the study of scripture and drew inspiration from the lives and teachings of saints and theologians. The wisdom and insights gained from these texts influenced her understanding of God and guided her in her religious practices.

These influences and religious experiences helped shape St. Bridget's unique spiritual perspective and informed her teachings and writings. They fueled her commitment to a life of deep prayer, contemplation, and devotion to God. Her encounters with the divine and her engagement with various religious practices and traditions played a vital role in her journey to becoming a revered mystic and religious leader in medieval Europe.

Chapter Two

A Life Transformed

2.1 Spiritual awakening and devotion

St. Bridget's spiritual awakening and her deep devotion to God were central to her life and played a transformative role in shaping her journey as a mystic and religious leader. Her profound spiritual experiences and unwavering commitment to her faith propelled her to seek a closer relationship with God and to dedicate her life to serving Him. Here is a closer look at St. Bridget's spiritual awakening and devotion:

. Mystical Experiences: St. Bridget's spiritual journey was marked by extraordinary mystical experiences. From an early age, she claimed to receive divine revelations and vivid visions, which she believed were messages from God. These experiences deepened her sense of the divine presence and ignited a passionate desire to know and serve God more fully.

2. Intimacy with God: St. Bridget cultivated a deep sense of intimacy with God through prayer and contemplation. She sought solitude and silence to commune with Him, fostering a personal and profound connection. Through these practices, she developed a heightened awareness of God' love and guidance in her life.

3. Devotion to Christ's Passion: St. Bridget had a profound devotion to the suffering and sacrifice of Jesus Christ. She meditated on the Passion of Christ, contemplating His love and the redemptive power of His sacrifice. This devotion fueled her own sacrificial love and commitment to serving others.

4. Love for the Eucharist: St. Bridget had a deep reverence for the Eucharist viewing it as the true presence of Christ. She experienced a profound spiritual union with Jesus during the reception of the Holy Communion which strengthened her devotion and nourished her soul.

5. Prayer and Contemplation: St. Bridget dedicated significant time to prayer and contemplation, seeking to deepen her understanding of God' will and to align her life with His purposes. She engaged in personal and communal prayers, often spending extended periods in fervent dialogue with God. Her prayer life was characterized by humility, reverence, and deep longing for spiritual growth.

6. Penitential Practices: St. Bridget embraced penitential practices as a means of purifying her soul and expressing her love and contrition for her sins. She fasted, practiced self-denial, and engaged in acts of charity and service to the poor and marginalized. These penitential practices were a manifestation of her deep devotion and desire for spiritual transformation.

7. Spiritual Gifts and Discernment: St. Bridget's spiritual awakening endowed her with spiritual gifts, including the ability to discern the authenticity of visions and revelations. She relied on her discernment to discern the true nature of her mystical experiences and to discern God's will in her life.

St. Bridget's spiritual awakening and her unwavering devotion to God guided her on a transformative journey of faith. Her experiences of divine presence, her devotion to Christ's Passion, her love for the Eucharist, and her commitment to prayer and contemplation shaped her understanding of the spiritual life and fueled her passionate pursuit of God. These experiences and her deep devotion to God became the driving forces behind her subsequent religious endeavors and her influential role as a mystic and religious leader.

2.2 Visions and divine encounters

St. Bridget of Sweden's life was marked by numerous visions and divine encounters, which played a significant role in shaping her spiritual journey and influencing her teachings. These mystical experiences provided her with profound insights into the divine realm and deepened her connection with God. Here are some key aspects of St. Bridget's visions and divine encounters:

1. Early Visions: St. Bridget began experiencing visions and revelations from a young age. At the age of seven, she had her first mystical encounter when she saw a vision of Jesus Christ crucified. This early vision instilled in her a deep sense of awe and reverence for the suffering of Christ.

2. Dialogue with Christ: St. Bridget's visions often involved direct conversations with Jesus Christ. She described these encounters as intimate and personal, where Christ would communicate His teachings, messages of love, and guidance to her. These dialogues with Christ shaped her understanding of His teachings and formed the basis of her spiritual insights.

3. The Nativity Vision: One of the most renowned visions of St. Bridget was her vivid experience of the Nativity. In this vision, she saw the scene of Christ's birth in Bethlehem, witnessing the humility, love, and divine

presence surrounding the event. This vision deepened her devotion to the Incarnation and the significance of Christ's birth.

4. Revelations of Heaven and Hell: St. Bridget had visions and revelations of both heaven and hell. She described the glory and joy of heaven, as well as the suffering and torment of hell. These visions served as a reminder of the consequences of sin and the ultimate reward of eternal life with God.

5. Divine Instructions for Religious Reform: St. Bridget received divine instructions and messages from God, urging her to advocate for religious reform and the restoration of faith. She was called to challenge corruption, immorality, and abuses within the Church and society. These messages influenced her writings and her interactions with religious and political leaders.

6. Visits from Saints and Angels: St. Bridget also reported encounters with saints and angels in her visions. She described receiving guidance, teachings, and comfort from these celestial beings. These encounters reinforced her faith and provided her with spiritual companionship.

7. Visions of the Crucifixion: St. Bridget frequently had visions of Christ's Passion and the crucifixion. These visions deepened her understanding of Christ's sacrifice and fueled her devotion to the redemptive power of His

suffering. She often emphasized the importance of meditating on the Passion and the love that motivated Christ's sacrifice.

St. Bridget's visions and divine encounters served as a source of spiritual guidance, inspiration, and authority. These experiences allowed her to communicate profound insights and teachings to others, emphasizing the importance of faith, repentance, and living in accordance with God's will. They shaped her understanding of God's love, the path of salvation, and the necessity of personal transformation. Through her visions, St. Bridget offered a glimpse into the divine realm, inspiring others to deepen their faith and seek a closer relationship with God.

2.3 Decision to dedicate her life to God

St. Bridget's decision to dedicate her life to God was a pivotal moment that set the course for her remarkable spiritual journey and her subsequent role as a religious leader. Her deep faith, spiritual experiences, and encounters with God influenced her decision to commit herself fully to a life of service and devotion. Here is an exploration of the factors that contributed to St. Bridget's decision to dedicate her life to God:

1. Spiritual Awakening: St. Bridget's early mystical experiences and visions served as a catalyst for her spiritual awakening. These encounters deepened

her awareness of God's presence, kindled her love for Him, and heightened her desire to live a life aligned with His will.

2. Personal Relationship with God: St. Bridget developed a profound personal relationship with God through prayer, contemplation, and dialogue. Through these spiritual practices, she grew in intimacy with God and experienced His love and guidance. This personal relationship fueled her desire to dedicate herself fully to God's service.

3. Commitment to Christian Values: St. Bridget's upbringing within a devout Christian family instilled in her a deep commitment to Christian values. She recognized the importance of living a life of virtue, compassion, and selflessness. Her decision to dedicate herself to God was a natural extension of her desire to live out these values fully.

4. Influence of Religious Role Models: St. Bridget was influenced by the examples of other devout individuals who had devoted their lives to God. The lives of saints, mystics, and religious figures she encountered in her studies and spiritual experiences inspired her and provided models of deep commitment and holiness.

5. Discernment and Guidance: St. Bridget sought guidance from trusted spiritual directors and advisors, who helped her discern God's calling in her

life. Through their counsel and support, she gained clarity and confirmation in her decision to dedicate herself to God.

6. Love for Christ and Desire for Union: St. Bridget's profound love for Jesus Christ and her longing for spiritual union with Him were driving forces behind her decision. She desired to deepen her relationship with Christ, to align her life completely with His teachings, and to participate in His redemptive work.

7. Sense of Mission and Calling: St. Bridget felt a strong sense of mission and calling to contribute to the renewal of the Church and society. She believed that God had entrusted her with a purpose to advocate for reform and to guide others on their spiritual journeys.

Ultimately, St. Bridget's decision to dedicate her life to God emerged from a deep yearning for a closer relationship with Him, a commitment to Christian values, the influence of role models, and a sense of mission and calling. This decision would shape the rest of her life, leading her to establish the Bridgettine Order, engage in works of charity and reform, and leave a lasting legacy as a revered mystic and religious leader.

Chapter Three

Founding the Bridgettine Order

3.1 Inspiration and calling

St. Bridget of Sweden was inspired and called to a life of devotion, service, and reform through various influences and divine revelations. These inspirations and callings guided her spiritual journey and shaped her significant contributions as a mystic and religious leader. Here are some key aspects of St. Bridget's inspiration and calling:

1. Divine Revelations: St. Bridget experienced numerous visions and divine revelations from a young age. These encounters with the divine provided her with insights into God's will and the mission He had for her. Through these revelations, she gained a deeper understanding of the love, mercy, and justice of God, which fueled her passion to spread His message.

2. Love for Christ: St. Bridget had a profound love for Jesus Christ, which inspired her to emulate His teachings and follow His example. She was

deeply moved by Christ's suffering, sacrifice, and unconditional love for humanity. Her love for Christ motivated her to devote her life to Him and to share His message of love and redemption.

3. Desire for Union with God: St. Bridget yearned for a deep and intimate union with God. She longed to experience His presence and to be united with Him in mind, heart, and spirit. This desire for union with God was a driving force in her life and influenced her spiritual practices and teachings.

4. Spiritual Role Models: St. Bridget was inspired by the examples of other holy individuals who devoted their lives to God. She studied the lives and teachings of saints, mystics, and religious figures, drawing inspiration from their profound faith, selflessness, and commitment to God. Their examples served as a source of encouragement and guidance for her own spiritual journey.

5. Divine Calling for Reform: St. Bridget received divine messages and calling to advocate for reform within the Church and society. She was directed to challenge corruption, immorality, and abuses, and to encourage renewal and adherence to the teachings of Christ. This calling drove her to confront social injustices, promote moral values, and encourage a deeper commitment to God.

6. Spiritual Guidance: St. Bridget sought spiritual guidance from trusted advisors, including Peter Olivi, a renowned theologian, and her confessor, Master Matthias. Through their counsel and support, she gained clarity and affirmation of her calling. Their guidance helped her discern God's will and provided direction for her spiritual journey.

7. Passion for Salvation and the Salvation of Souls: St. Bridget had a deep concern for the salvation of souls. She was inspired by a genuine desire to lead others to God, to help them embrace His love and mercy, and to guide them on the path to eternal life. This passion for salvation motivated her to teach, write, and engage in acts of charity, all with the intention of leading others closer to God.

St. Bridget's inspiration and calling stemmed from divine revelations, a profound love for Christ, a desire for union with God, the influence of spiritual role models, a divine calling for reform, and a passion for the salvation of souls. These inspirations and callings drove her to dedicate her life to God and to leave a lasting impact on the spiritual landscape of her time. Her teachings, writings, and works of charity continue to inspire and guide countless individuals seeking a deeper connection with God and a life of devotion and service.

3.2 Challenges and obstacles

St. Bridget of Sweden faced numerous challenges and obstacles throughout her life as she pursued her spiritual calling and worked towards the reforms she believed were necessary. These challenges tested her faith, perseverance, and determination. Here are some of the challenges and obstacles that St. Bridget encountered:

1. Opposition from Church Authorities: St. Bridget's reform-minded ideas and her calls for moral and institutional change within the Church were met with resistance and opposition from some Church authorities. Her outspokenness and criticisms of corruption and abuses within the Church were not universally welcomed, and she faced skepticism and resistance from those who were resistant to change.

2. Political Instability: The political landscape of medieval Europe during St. Bridget's time was marked by frequent conflicts and power struggles. She lived during a period of political instability, with shifting alliances and competing factions. These tumultuous circumstances could pose challenges to her work and cause disruptions in her efforts to advocate for reform.

3. Papal Schism: St. Bridget witnessed the Papal Schism, a period in which rival claimants vied for the papacy, resulting in divisions and conflicts within the Catholic Church. This schism complicated matters and hindered

efforts for unity and reform. St. Bridget navigated the complexities of this fractured ecclesiastical landscape and sought to address the challenges it presented.

4. Financial Constraints: Establishing and maintaining the Bridgettine Order and carrying out charitable works required financial resources. St. Bridget faced financial constraints and had to rely on the generosity of others to support her endeavors. At times, securing sufficient resources for her projects and charitable activities proved to be a challenge.

5. Resistance to Change: St. Bridget's ideas for reform challenged long-established practices and societal norms. Her calls for moral renewal, social justice, and changes within the Church met resistance from those who were comfortable with the status quo. Overcoming resistance to change and convincing others of the need for reform required perseverance and persuasive efforts on her part.

6. Personal Loss and Tragedy: St. Bridget faced personal loss and tragedy in her life, including the deaths of loved ones, including her husband and some of her children. These losses undoubtedly presented emotional challenges and required her to find strength and resilience in the face of personal grief.

7. Persecution and Exile: St. Bridget faced persecution and criticism for he outspokenness and her efforts to bring about change. At times, sh encountered opposition and hostility, leading to periods of exile an isolation. These periods of exile presented additional challenges to her wor and required her to navigate uncertain and often difficult circumstances.

Despite these challenges and obstacles, St. Bridget demonstrate remarkable determination, resilience, and faith. She persisted in her pursui of reform, continued her charitable works, and remained committed to he spiritual calling. Her unwavering dedication to her beliefs and her ability t overcome adversity continue to inspire people today.

3.3 Establishing the first convent

St. Bridget of Sweden played a significant role in the establishment of th first convent of the Bridgettine Order, also known as the Order of the Mos Holy Savior. This endeavor faced various challenges and required he determination, perseverance, and the support of others. Here is an overviev of the process and challenges involved in establishing the first convent:

1. Vision and Divine Inspiration: St. Bridget's vision for establishing religious order was rooted in her profound spiritual experiences an encounters with God. Through divine revelations, she received guidanc

and instructions to found a contemplative and active religious community dedicated to prayer, study, and charitable works.

2. Papal Approval: St. Bridget sought papal approval for the establishment of the Bridgettine Order. She approached Pope Urban V and presented her vision and plans. Obtaining papal approval was crucial for the legitimacy and recognition of the order. However, it took several years and persistent efforts before she received formal approval from the Pope.

3. Recruitment of Members: Once the order received papal approval, St. Bridget began the process of recruiting women who were interested in joining the religious community. She attracted women from various backgrounds, including noble and common families, who shared her vision and desired to dedicate their lives to God through the Bridgettine way of life.

4. Acquisition of Property: Finding suitable property for the convent posed a challenge. St. Bridget sought a location that would accommodate the needs of the community and provide a suitable environment for prayer and contemplation. Eventually, she acquired the former palace of the governor of Rome, which became the site of the first Bridgettine convent, known as the House of St. Savior.

5. Infrastructure and Organizational Development: Establishing the convent involved setting up the necessary infrastructure and organizational structures. St. Bridget designed the layout of the convent, which included spaces for prayer, study, living quarters, and areas for communal activities. She also established rules and guidelines for the religious life and governance of the community.

6. Financial Support: Financing the establishment and maintenance of the convent was a significant challenge. St. Bridget relied on the generosity of benefactors and donations to fund the construction, maintenance, and ongoing operations of the convent. She reached out to individuals, including royalty and influential figures, to seek financial support for the Bridgettine Order.

7. Overcoming Opposition: Establishing the first Bridgettine convent faced opposition and skepticism from those who questioned the need for a new religious order. Some Church authorities and individuals resisted the reforms and changes advocated by St. Bridget. Overcoming this opposition required her persistence, persuasive efforts, and the support of those who believed in her vision.

Despite the challenges, St. Bridget's determination and the support she received led to the successful establishment of the first Bridgettine convent. This marked the beginning of the Bridgettine Order, which would grow and spread to various locations across Europe, promoting a combination of contemplative and active religious life, centered on prayer, study, and charitable works. St. Bridget's pioneering efforts in establishing the first convent laid the foundation for the continued influence and impact of the Bridgettine Order throughout history.

Chapter Four

Teachings and Writings

4.1 The spiritual insights of St. Bridget

St. Bridget of Sweden was known for her profound spiritual insights, which she expressed through her teachings, writings, and revelations. Her spiritual insights were deeply rooted in her personal experiences, her encounters with God, and her understanding of Scripture. Here are some of the spiritual insights of St. Bridget:

1. Divine Love and Mercy: St. Bridget emphasized the boundless love and mercy of God. She taught that God's love is unconditional and that His mercy is available to all who turn to Him with contrite hearts. She believed in the transformative power of God's love and mercy to bring healing, forgiveness, and salvation.

2. Union with God: St. Bridget sought a deep union with God and taught the importance of cultivating an intimate relationship with Him. She

ncouraged others to engage in prayer, contemplation, and the sacraments s means to experience a profound connection with the divine. She believed hat true happiness and fulfillment are found in communion with God.

. Meditation on the Passion: St. Bridget had a deep devotion to the Passion f Christ. She emphasized the significance of meditating on Christ's uffering and sacrifice as a means of understanding His immense love for umanity. She believed that contemplating the Passion could inspire ratitude, repentance, and a desire for greater conformity to Christ's selfless ove.

. Repentance and Conversion: St. Bridget emphasized the importance of epentance and conversion. She called upon individuals to examine their ives, acknowledge their sins, and turn back to God in sincere repentance. he believed that true repentance brings about inner transformation and pens the way for God's grace and forgiveness.

. Moral and Social Reform: St. Bridget advocated for moral and social eform within the Church and society. She challenged corruption, injustice, nd immorality, urging individuals to live lives of virtue, justice, and ompassion. She believed in the responsibility of both religious and secular eaders to foster a just and loving society.

6. The Value of Humility: St. Bridget emphasized the importance o humility in the spiritual life. She taught that true greatness is found i humility and that humility opens the way for God's grace and transformativ power. She encouraged others to imitate Christ's humility, considerin others as more important than oneself.

7. Eternal Life and Heaven: St. Bridget provided insights into the realitie of eternal life and the joys of heaven. She shared visions and revelations o the glory and happiness awaiting the faithful in heaven. She stressed th importance of living with an eternal perspective, striving for holiness, an keeping heaven as the ultimate goal.

St. Bridget's spiritual insights were shaped by her personal encounters wit God, her deep understanding of Scripture, and her desire to guide others o the path of holiness. Her teachings and writings continue to inspire an encourage individuals to seek a deeper relationship with God, to live live of virtue and love, and to strive for eternal union with Him.

4.2 Her written works and their impact

St. Bridget of Sweden was a prolific writer, and her written works had significant impact on the religious and cultural landscape of her time an beyond. Her writings, which included revelations, prayers, and instruction:

were influential in promoting spiritual growth, moral reform, and devotion to God. Here are some of her written works and their impact:

1. Revelations: St. Bridget recorded her divine revelations in a collection known as the "Revelations of St. Bridget." These revelations provided insights into the divine realm, teachings on various spiritual topics, and messages of love, mercy, and repentance. They had a profound impact on the faithful, inspiring them to deepen their faith, pursue holiness, and seek a closer relationship with God.

2. Prayers and Devotions: St. Bridget composed prayers and devotions, many of which were compiled in a prayer book known as the "Prayers of St. Bridget." These prayers, which reflected her deep spirituality and love for God, became popular among the faithful. They were embraced as powerful tools for personal prayer, meditation, and spiritual growth. St. Bridget's prayers continue to be treasured and recited by individuals seeking spiritual connection and guidance.

3. Writings on Moral and Social Reform: St. Bridget wrote extensively on moral and social reform, addressing issues such as corruption, immorality, and injustice within the Church and society. Her writings challenged individuals, especially those in positions of power and authority, to embrace righteousness, justice, and compassion. Her calls for reform resonated with many and contributed to discussions on improving the Church and society.

4. Spiritual Instructions and Guidance: St. Bridget provided practical and spiritual instructions for the faithful in her writings. She emphasized the importance of virtues, the practice of self-discipline, and the pursuit of holiness. Her writings provided guidance on prayer, sacraments, and living a Christian life in various circumstances. They served as a source of inspiration and practical advice for individuals seeking to deepen their faith and grow in their spiritual journey.

5. Influence on Religious Orders: St. Bridget's writings had a significant impact on religious orders, particularly the Bridgettine Order that she founded. Her spiritual insights and teachings formed the basis of the order's spirituality, guiding its members in their pursuit of prayer, contemplation, and works of charity. Her writings also influenced other religious communities, inspiring them to prioritize devotion to God, adherence to religious vows, and the pursuit of holiness.

6. Influence on Devotional Literature: St. Bridget's writings had a lasting impact on devotional literature. Her profound spiritual experiences, revelations, and prayers inspired other writers and mystics, who drew from her works in their own writings. Her influence can be seen in subsequent devotional literature, particularly in medieval and Renaissance periods.

St. Bridget's written works continue to be studied, cherished, and utilized by individuals seeking spiritual growth and guidance. Her insights, teachings, and prayers have had a lasting impact on the faithful, shaping their understanding of God, their approach to prayer, and their commitment to a life of holiness. Her writings remain a testament to her deep faith, her love for God, and her desire to lead others closer to Him.

4.3 Influence on medieval spirituality

St. Bridget of Sweden had a profound influence on medieval spirituality, leaving a lasting impact on the religious and cultural landscape of her time. Her spiritual teachings, writings, and example inspired countless individuals, both within and beyond the confines of religious orders. Here are some key ways in which St. Bridget influenced medieval spirituality:

1. Mystical Spirituality: St. Bridget's mystical experiences and revelations contributed to the flourishing of mystical spirituality in the medieval period. Her visions, dialogues with God, and deep insights into the divine realm resonated with individuals seeking a direct and personal experience of God. Her writings and teachings on mystical topics encouraged others to pursue a contemplative and experiential approach to spirituality.

2. Devotion to Christ: St. Bridget's intense devotion to the person of Jesus Christ had a profound impact on medieval spirituality. Her meditations on the Passion, her emphasis on Christ's suffering and sacrificial love, and her teachings on the Eucharist deepened the devotion of the faithful to Christ.

Her writings inspired a greater focus on the humanity and divinity of Christ, fostering a personal and emotional connection with Him.

3. Emphasis on Repentance and Conversion: St. Bridget's teachings on repentance and conversion resonated with the medieval mindset, which was characterized by a strong sense of sin and the need for redemption. Her emphasis on sincere repentance, the transformative power of God's mercy, and the necessity of personal conversion spoke to the spiritual concerns and aspirations of the time. Her writings provided practical guidance for individuals seeking a path of repentance and spiritual renewal.

4. Moral Reform and Social Justice: St. Bridget's writings on moral reform and social justice challenged the prevalent abuses and corruption within the Church and society. Her calls for righteousness, honesty, and compassion inspired individuals to pursue a more ethical and just way of life. Her influence contributed to a growing awareness of the need for moral reform and the promotion of social justice within medieval society.

5. Bridgettine Spirituality: The establishment of the Bridgettine Order by St. Bridget introduced a new form of religious life that combined contemplation, liturgical prayer, and active works of charity. The Bridgettine spirituality, based on St. Bridget's teachings and example, became influential among other religious orders and individuals seeking a balanced approach to the spiritual life. The order's focus on prayer,

ommunity, and service to others impacted the broader understanding and
racticc of medieval spirituality.

. Devotional Literature: St. Bridget's writings, particularly her prayers and
neditations, inspired a rich tradition of devotional literature in the medieval
eriod. Her personal prayers, reflections on the life of Christ, and teachings
n the virtues influenced subsequent writers and mystics who sought to
xpress their own devotion and deepen their spiritual lives. St. Bridget's
levotional works became models for expressing personal piety and
levotion to God.

t. Bridget of Sweden's influence on medieval spirituality was far-reaching
nd enduring. Her emphasis on personal experience of God, devotion to
Christ, calls for repentance and moral reform, and the establishment of the
3ridgettine Order left an indelible mark on the spiritual landscape of the
ime. Her writings and teachings continue to inspire and shape the spiritual
ives of individuals seeking a deeper relationship with God and a more
neaningful engagement with the Christian faith.

Chapter Five

Pilgrimage and Travel

5.1 Journeys and pilgrimages undertaken by St Bridget

St. Bridget of Sweden embarked on several significant journeys an pilgrimages throughout her life. These journeys provided her wit opportunities for spiritual growth, encounters with importan religious figures, and deepened her understanding of the Christian faith Here are some of the notable journeys and pilgrimages undertaken by S Bridget:

1. Pilgrimage to Santiago de Compostela: St. Bridget made a pilgrimage t the renowned shrine of Santiago de Compostela in Spain. This pilgrimag was a significant undertaking during the medieval period and allowed he to immerse herself in the rich spiritual traditions and history associated wit the pilgrimage route. It provided her with an opportunity for praye reflection, and encounters with fellow pilgrims.

2. Pilgrimage to the Holy Land: St. Bridget embarked on a pilgrimage to the Holy Land, including Jerusalem, Bethlehem, and other significant biblical sites. This pilgrimage was a deeply meaningful journey for her, as it allowed her to walk in the footsteps of Christ and experience firsthand the places central to Christian faith and history. It deepened her understanding of the life and teachings of Jesus Christ.

3. Pilgrimage to Rome: St. Bridget made several pilgrimages to Rome, the center of Catholicism. Rome held immense spiritual significance for St. Bridget, and she sought to visit the tombs of the apostles and other holy sites. These pilgrimages allowed her to deepen her connection with the universal Church and to engage with the religious and political leaders of the time.

4. Pilgrimage to Vadstena: After returning from her journeys to Santiago de Compostela, the Holy Land, and Rome, St. Bridget made a pilgrimage to Vadstena, Sweden. It was during this pilgrimage that she received a divine revelation instructing her to establish a religious community in Vadstena, which eventually led to the founding of the Bridgettine Order.

5. Journeys within Europe: St. Bridget undertook several journeys within Europe to advocate for religious reform and to seek support for her endeavors. She traveled to various cities and courts, including Avignon and Naples, where she met with popes, cardinals, and political leaders. These

journeys allowed her to share her spiritual insights, promote her reform agenda, and gain support for her religious community.

These journeys and pilgrimages undertaken by St. Bridget provided her with opportunities for spiritual enrichment, encounters with important religious figures, and the deepening of her faith. They allowed her to connect with the broader Christian tradition, gain insights into the history and teachings of the Church, and contribute to the reform efforts of her time. The experiences and encounters from her journeys and pilgrimages significantly shaped her spiritual journey and her contributions to the religious landscape of medieval Europe.

5.2 Encounters with other spiritual leaders

St. Bridget of Sweden had several significant encounters with other spiritual leaders and influential figures of her time. These encounters provided her with guidance, affirmation, and the opportunity to engage in discussions on matters of faith, reform, and spiritual growth. Here are some notable encounters St. Bridget had with other spiritual leaders:

1. Encounter with Saint Catherine of Sweden: St. Bridget's daughter, Catherine, became a nun and was known for her holiness. St. Bridget had numerous spiritual conversations and exchanges with her daughter, who provided her with spiritual guidance and support. St. Bridget valued

Catherine's insights and considered her a source of inspiration in her own spiritual journey.

2. Meeting with Pope Urban V: St. Bridget had an audience with Pope Urban V during one of her visits to Rome. She sought papal approval for the establishment of the Bridgettine Order and shared her visions, revelations, and ideas for reform. Pope Urban V recognized St. Bridget's sanctity and spiritual wisdom, granting her support and approval for her religious endeavors.

3. Correspondence with Peter Olivi: St. Bridget engaged in a correspondence with Peter Olivi, a prominent Franciscan theologian of her time. They exchanged letters discussing theological matters, spiritual insights, and the need for moral and religious reform. St. Bridget valued Peter Olivi's scholarly knowledge and his commitment to a more authentic and heartfelt expression of faith.

4. Interaction with Master Matthias: Master Matthias, St. Bridget's confessor and advisor, played an instrumental role in her spiritual journey. He provided her with guidance, interpreted her visions and revelations, and supported her in her reform efforts. Master Matthias accompanied St. Bridget on some of her journeys and served as a spiritual mentor throughout her life.

5. Dialogue with Christ: St. Bridget's mystical experiences included direct conversations with Jesus Christ. Through these dialogues, she received spiritual teachings, insights, and guidance from the Lord. These encounters with Christ served as a profound source of spiritual direction and strengthened her faith in her mission.

These encounters with spiritual leaders and figures allowed St. Bridget to exchange ideas, seek guidance, and receive affirmation in her spiritual journey and reform efforts. The insights and support she gained from these encounters contributed to her own spiritual growth, deepened her understanding of the faith, and strengthened her commitment to promoting spiritual renewal and moral reform.

5.3 Impacts of her travels on her spiritual journey

St. Bridget of Sweden's travels had a significant impact on her spiritual journey, shaping her understanding of the faith, deepening her relationship with God, and inspiring her to pursue her mission of reform and devotion. Here are some of the impacts of her travels on her spiritual journey:

1. Experiential Knowledge: St. Bridget's travels allowed her to visit significant religious sites, including pilgrimage destinations and holy places associated with the life of Christ. These firsthand experiences provided her with a tangible connection to the historical and spiritual aspects of the faith.

Walking in the footsteps of Christ, witnessing sacred artifacts, and engaging with the local religious communities enriched her understanding of the Christian tradition and deepened her faith.

2. Encounter with Different Spiritual Traditions: Through her travels, St. Bridget encountered diverse spiritual traditions, practices, and expressions of faith. These encounters exposed her to different religious customs, spiritual insights, and theological perspectives. Engaging with individuals from various backgrounds broadened her spiritual horizons and allowed her to gain a deeper appreciation for the universality of the Christian faith.

3. Guidance from Spiritual Leaders: During her travels, St. Bridget had the opportunity to meet with and receive guidance from spiritual leaders, including popes, theologians, and other influential figures. These encounters provided her with wisdom, affirmation, and spiritual direction. The counsel she received from these leaders helped shape her understanding of the faith, validated her spiritual experiences, and provided the support she needed to pursue her mission.

4. Confirmation of Divine Revelations: St. Bridget's travels often included encounters with individuals who recognized the authenticity and significance of her divine revelations. These encounters served as a confirmation of her mystical experiences and the messages she received

from God. The affirmation she received from spiritual leaders and fellow believers bolstered her confidence in her spiritual journey and mission.

5. Inspiration for Reform and Devotion: The exposure to different religious communities, practices, and traditions during her travels inspired St. Bridget in her quest for reform and devotion. Witnessing the dedication and devotion of fellow pilgrims, the work of religious orders, and the vibrancy of spiritual life in different places fueled her own commitment to promote a deeper spiritual life, moral reform, and devotion to Christ.

6. Strengthened Commitment to Pilgrimage and Devotion: St. Bridget's travels reinforced her belief in the power of pilgrimage as a means of spiritual growth and connection with God. Her own experiences during her journeys deepened her appreciation for the value of visiting sacred sites, engaging in prayerful reflection, and participating in devotional practices. This strengthened her commitment to pilgrimage and inspired her to encourage others to embark on similar spiritual journeys.

Overall, St. Bridget's travels had a profound impact on her spiritual journey. They enriched her understanding of the faith, exposed her to different spiritual traditions, and provided her with guidance, affirmation, and inspiration. Her experiences during her travels deepened her relationship with God, fueled her passion for reform and devotion, and shaped her mission as a mystic and religious leader.

Chapter Six

Interactions with Kings and Popes

6.1 Relationships with royalty

St. Bridget of Sweden had significant relationships with members of royalty during her lifetime. Her interactions with royalty played a role in shaping her spiritual journey, influencing her reform efforts, and providing support for her religious endeavors. Here are some notable relationships St. Bridget had with royalty:

1. Queen Blanche of Namur: St. Bridget served as a lady-in-waiting to Queen Blanche of Namur, who was the wife of King Magnus II of Sweden. Queen Blanche valued St. Bridget's spiritual counsel and trusted her as a confidante. St. Bridget's association with Queen Blanche provided her with opportunities to advocate for moral and religious reform within the royal court.

2. King Magnus II of Sweden: St. Bridget had a personal connection with King Magnus II of Sweden, who supported her spiritual endeavors and reform efforts. King Magnus and St. Bridget had discussions about religious matters, and he sought her guidance and prayers. St. Bridget's relationship with King Magnus allowed her to influence him in matters of faith and morality.

3. King Birger of Sweden: St. Bridget's relationship with King Birger of Sweden was more contentious. She spoke out against his immoral behavior and unjust actions, advocating for moral reform and the promotion of social justice. St. Bridget challenged King Birger to rule with righteousness and to prioritize the welfare of his subjects. Her criticisms and confrontations with the king reflected her commitment to upholding Christian values.

4. Queen Philippa of England: St. Bridget maintained correspondence with Queen Philippa of England, who was the wife of King Edward III. They exchanged letters discussing matters of faith, spirituality, and devotion. St. Bridget's relationship with Queen Philippa provided her with a connection to the English royal court and opportunities to share her spiritual insights and teachings.

5. Queen Joan of Naples: St. Bridget visited Queen Joan of Naples during her travels and engaged in spiritual discussions with her. Queen Joan respected St. Bridget's spiritual wisdom and sought her guidance on matters

of faith. Their conversations provided St. Bridget with an opportunity to influence a prominent royal figure and advocate for religious reform.

St. Bridget's relationships with royalty allowed her to have a significant impact on the spiritual lives of monarchs and influence their decisions in matters of faith and morality. Her interactions with royalty provided her with a platform to advocate for reform, address social issues, and promote a deeper commitment to the Christian faith. St. Bridget's influence on members of royalty contributed to her broader efforts to bring about spiritual renewal and moral reform within the Church and society.

6.2 Influence on political and religious leaders

St. Bridget of Sweden exerted a notable influence on political and religious leaders of her time. Her spiritual insights, moral teachings, and commitment to reform resonated with those in positions of power, and her counsel and guidance were sought by both political and religious figures. Here are some ways in which St. Bridget influenced political and religious leaders:

1. Influence on Kings and Queens: St. Bridget had interactions with several monarchs, including King Magnus II of Sweden, Queen Blanche of Namur, King Birger of Sweden, Queen Philippa of England, and Queen Joan of Naples. Through her conversations, writings, and personal encounters, she challenged them to rule with justice, uphold Christian values, and promote

social welfare. Her counsel and spiritual insights influenced their decision-making and moral conduct.

2. Advisors to Political Leaders: St. Bridget acted as an advisor to political leaders and offered guidance on matters of governance, justice, and social responsibility. Her teachings emphasized the importance of rulers seeking divine guidance, ruling with righteousness, and prioritizing the welfare of their subjects. Political leaders sought her counsel for both spiritual and practical matters.

3. Influence on Church Authorities: St. Bridget's calls for moral reform and renewal within the Church resonated with Church authorities. She engaged in discussions with popes, cardinals, and theologians, offering her insights and sharing her visions and revelations. Her influence contributed to discussions on the need for spiritual renewal, adherence to Christian values, and the promotion of social justice within the Church.

4. Advocacy for Religious Reform: St. Bridget actively advocated for religious reform, challenging corruption and immorality within the Church. Her writings and teachings on the need for moral renewal influenced religious leaders, encouraging them to examine their own practices and embrace a more authentic expression of faith. St. Bridget's reform-minded approach inspired religious leaders to prioritize spiritual growth, adherence to religious vows, and the pursuit of holiness.

. Dialogue with Papal Authorities: St. Bridget had personal encounters and correspondences with several popes, including Pope Urban V and Pope Gregory XI. These interactions allowed her to share her spiritual insights, reform ideas, and visions. Popes sought her guidance and prayers, recognizing her sanctity and wisdom. St. Bridget's influence on papal authorities contributed to discussions on reform and spiritual renewal within the Church.

St. Bridget's influence on political and religious leaders was rooted in her spiritual depth, moral teachings, and commitment to reform. Her interactions with leaders provided a platform for sharing her insights and challenging them to uphold Christian values in their roles of authority. Her influence extended beyond individual leaders and contributed to broader discussions on spiritual renewal, moral reform, and social justice within both political and religious spheres.

5.3 Advocacy for social justice and reforms

St. Bridget of Sweden was a passionate advocate for social justice and various reforms during her time. Her deep commitment to the Christian faith and her understanding of the Gospel teachings fueled her desire to address societal injustices, promote ethical behavior, and advocate for the well-being of the marginalized. Here are some of the areas where St. Bridget advocated for social justice and reforms:

1. Opposition to Corruption: St. Bridget strongly denounced corruption within the Church and society. She called for transparency, integrity, and accountability among religious and political leaders. Her writings and teachings emphasized the importance of ethical conduct, denouncing bribery, nepotism, and the misuse of power. St. Bridget challenged those in authority to uphold their responsibilities with honesty and fairness.

2. Care for the Poor and Needy: St. Bridget had a deep concern for the well being of the poor, needy, and marginalized. She advocated for their rights calling on society to provide for their basic needs and offer them compassion and support. St. Bridget encouraged acts of charity and practical assistance to alleviate the suffering and injustice faced by the vulnerable.

3. Reform of Monastic Life: St. Bridget saw the need for reform within monastic life, particularly the Bridgettine Order she founded. She emphasized the importance of adherence to religious vows, simplicity of lifestyle, and a focus on prayer, contemplation, and acts of charity. St Bridget encouraged her fellow religious to live with humility, renounce materialism, and prioritize their spiritual calling.

4. Promoting Morality and Family Values: St. Bridget stressed the importance of moral values and strong family bonds. She advocated for fidelity in marriages, the proper upbringing of children, and the fostering of

healthy and virtuous relationships. St. Bridget's teachings emphasized the significance of integrity, faithfulness, and love within family units as the foundation for a just and harmonious society.

5. Advocacy for Women's Rights: St. Bridget recognized the value and dignity of women and advocated for their rights within the societal context of her time. She spoke out against the mistreatment and exploitation of women and called for their equal participation in society, education, and decision-making processes. St. Bridget challenged prevailing gender biases and sought to empower women to fulfill their potential.

6. Reforming Religious Practices: St. Bridget critiqued religious practices that had become empty rituals devoid of spiritual meaning. She emphasized the need for authentic devotion, heartfelt worship, and a genuine connection with God. St. Bridget encouraged a personal and transformative relationship with God, urging individuals to go beyond external observances and embrace a sincere faith.

St. Bridget's advocacy for social justice and reforms was driven by her deep faith, compassion for the marginalized, and her understanding of the Gospel's call to love and serve others. Her teachings, writings, and personal example continue to inspire individuals to work for social justice, to challenge corruption and inequality, and to foster a more just and compassionate society.

Chapter Seven

Legacy and Canonization

7.1 The enduring impact of St. Bridget's life and teachings

The life and teachings of St. Bridget of Sweden continue to have an enduring impact, leaving a profound legacy that extends beyond her lifetime. Here are some aspects of St. Bridget's life and teachings that continue to inspire and influence people today:

1. Spiritual Inspiration: St. Bridget's deep spirituality, her mystical experiences, and her unwavering devotion to God serve as a source of inspiration for individuals seeking a deeper relationship with the divine. Her teachings on prayer, contemplation, and union with God resonate with those who yearn for a more meaningful spiritual life.

2. Moral and Social Reform: St. Bridget's commitment to moral and social reform remains relevant today. Her advocacy for justice, integrity, and care

for the marginalized continues to inspire individuals and communities to work towards a more equitable and compassionate society. Her teachings challenge the status quo and call for a transformation of hearts and minds.

3. Bridgettine Order: The Bridgettine Order, founded by St. Bridget, continues to exist and carry on her spiritual legacy. The order's emphasis on prayer, contemplation, and active works of charity serves as a testament to St. Bridget's vision for religious life. The Bridgettine sisters and their contributions to the Church and society bear witness to her enduring impact.

4. Influence on Mystical Tradition: St. Bridget's mystical experiences and writings have had a lasting influence on the mystical tradition within Christianity. Her insights into the divine, her dialogues with Christ, and her teachings on union with God have inspired countless mystics and spiritual seekers throughout history.

5. Devotional Works: St. Bridget's prayers, meditations, and devotional writings continue to be cherished and utilized by individuals seeking spiritual nourishment. Her works, such as the "Revelations of St. Bridget" and the "Prayers of St. Bridget," provide a rich source of inspiration for personal prayer, reflection, and growth in the Christian faith.

6. Influence on Women: St. Bridget's example as a strong, influential woman in a time when women's voices were often marginalized or ignored continues to inspire women today. Her advocacy for women's rights, her leadership within the Bridgettine Order, and her influential interactions with political and religious leaders demonstrate the significant impact women can have in shaping society and the Church.

7. Canonization and Feast Day: St. Bridget's canonization by the Catholic Church in 1391 and the establishment of her feast day on July 23rd ensure that her life and teachings are officially recognized and celebrated within the liturgical calendar. This recognition contributes to the continued awareness and veneration of St. Bridget, keeping her memory and influence alive.

St. Bridget's life and teachings serve as a reminder of the transformative power of faith, the call to social justice, and the importance of a deep and personal relationship with God. Her enduring impact inspires individuals to seek holiness, pursue justice, and embrace a spirituality that engages both the mystical and the practical aspects of life.

7.2 Process of her canonization

The process of canonization for St. Bridget of Sweden involved several stages and required the examination of her life, writings, and reputation for sanctity. Here is a general overview of the process:

. Local Cult and Investigation: The process typically begins at the local level, where the individual is considered "venerable" based on a local cult or following that has developed around them. In St. Bridget's case, her reputation for holiness and the widespread veneration she received in Sweden provided the foundation for her cause of canonization.

. Formal Cause and Diocesan Investigation: Once the local cult has been established, a formal cause for canonization is initiated. This involves a diocesan investigation led by the bishop of the diocese where the individual lived and died. In St. Bridget's case, the Diocese of Linköping in Sweden conducted the investigation.

. Examination of Writings and Life: During the diocesan investigation, St. Bridget's writings, including her revelations and other spiritual works, were carefully examined. The purpose was to ensure the orthodoxy and authenticity of her teachings. Additionally, her life, virtues, and reputation for holiness were scrutinized to evaluate her suitability for canonization.

4. Beatification: If the diocesan investigation yields positive results, th cause moves forward to the next stage, which is beatification. The candidat is declared "blessed" by the Pope, recognizing that they are now among th blessed in heaven and may be venerated in a limited manner by the Church In St. Bridget's case, she was beatified by Pope Boniface IX in 1391.

5. Miracles and Canonization: Following beatification, the recognition o miracles attributed to the intercession of the individual is an essentia requirement for canonization. The miracles must be documentec thoroughly investigated, and verified as unexplainable by natural causes. I St. Bridget's case, multiple miracles were attributed to her intercession ove the years.

6. Formal Canonization: Once the required miracles are approved, the fina step is formal canonization, in which the individual is declared a saint b the Pope. St. Bridget was canonized by Pope Boniface IX in 139 recognizing her as a saint officially within the Catholic Church.

It is important to note that the canonization process has evolved over time and the specific steps and requirements can vary. The process is oversee by the Congregation for the Causes of Saints, a Vatican office responsibl for examining and evaluating candidates for sainthood.

St. Bridget's canonization attests to the recognition of her holiness, virtue, and the impact of her life and teachings on the faithful. Her canonization assures the faithful of her intercession and provides an official affirmation of her sanctity and the validity of her spiritual writings.

7.3 Devotion and veneration of St. Bridget over the centuries

The devotion and veneration of St. Bridget of Sweden have endured over the centuries, with her influence extending far beyond her lifetime. Here are some aspects of the devotion and veneration of St. Bridget:

1. Pilgrimages to Her Shrines: Pilgrims have traveled to the shrines associated with St. Bridget, particularly the Basilica of St. Bridget in Vadstena, Sweden, where her relics are enshrined. These pilgrimages offer an opportunity for the faithful to seek her intercession, deepen their faith, and pay homage to her life and holiness.

2. Bridgettine Order: The Bridgettine Order, founded by St. Bridget, has continued to exist and flourish. The order has houses and communities in various parts of the world, dedicated to prayer, contemplation, and acts of charity. The devotion and commitment of the Bridgettine sisters to St. Bridget's teachings serve as a testament to her ongoing influence.

3. Spread of Her Writings: St. Bridget's writings, including her revelations, prayers, and spiritual insights, have been widely disseminated and translated over the centuries. These writings continue to be treasured by the faithful, who find spiritual nourishment and guidance in her words. They serve as a source of devotion, inspiration, and contemplation for individuals seeking a deeper relationship with God.

4. Patronage and Intercession: St. Bridget is recognized as a patron saint of several causes, including Sweden, widows, and Europe. The faithful have invoked her intercession for various intentions, seeking her help and guidance in their spiritual journey, personal challenges, and concerns. Many attribute miracles and answered prayers to her intercession.

5. Feast Day Celebrations: The feast day of St. Bridget, July 23rd, is celebrated by the faithful around the world. Special liturgical services, processions, and devotional activities take place on this day, honoring her life, virtues, and contributions to the Church. These celebrations provide an opportunity for the faithful to deepen their connection with St. Bridget and seek her intercession.

6. Cultural Influence: St. Bridget's influence extends beyond religious devotion and into various aspects of culture. She has been the subject of art, literature, and music, with numerous artistic representations depicting scenes from her life and her spiritual encounters. These cultural expressions

serve to keep her memory alive and inspire others through the visual and literary arts.

The enduring devotion and veneration of St. Bridget of Sweden bear witness to the impact of her life, teachings, and holiness. Her continued presence in the hearts and minds of the faithful is a testament to her sanctity and the inspiration she provides to those who seek a deeper connection with God and a life of holiness.

7.4 Novena to St Bridget

Day 1:

O St. Bridget, faithful servant of God and model of virtue, intercede for us before the throne of grace. Obtain for us the grace to live a life of holiness and to follow Christ with unwavering devotion. Pray for us, O holy St. Bridget, and assist us in our spiritual journey. Amen.

Day 2:

O St. Bridget, who encountered Christ in your mystical experiences, teach us to seek His presence in our lives. Help us to deepen our prayer life and to grow in our relationship with our Lord. Pray for us, O holy St. Bridget, and lead us closer to Jesus. Amen.

Day 3:

O St. Bridget, who advocated for justice and cared for the marginalized, inspire us to work for a more just and compassionate society. Help us to recognize the dignity of every person and to strive for equality and fairness. Pray for us, O holy St. Bridget, and guide us in promoting social justice. Amen.

Day 4:

O St. Bridget, who embraced personal transformation and holiness, teach us to examine our lives and to embrace the process of growth and change. Help us to become the best versions of ourselves and to live according to God's will. Pray for us, O holy St. Bridget, and inspire us to seek holiness. Amen.

Day 5:

O St. Bridget, who fostered dialogue and understanding, intercede for us in our relationships and interactions with others. Help us to promote harmony, respect, and unity among all people, regardless of differences. Pray for us, O holy St. Bridget, and guide us in building bridges of love and understanding. Amen.

Day 6:

O St. Bridget, who empowered and supported others, teach us to use our gifts and talents for the benefit of those in need. Inspire us to be instruments of love, compassion, and service in our communities. Pray for us, O holy St. Bridget, and assist us in reaching out to others with generosity and kindness. Amen.

Day 7:

O St. Bridget, who lived a life of prayer and contemplation, intercede for us in our own spiritual journey. Help us to deepen our prayer life, to seek God's presence, and to find solace in His loving embrace. Pray for us, O holy St. Bridget, and guide us in our pursuit of a deeper relationship with God. Amen.

Day 8:

O St. Bridget, who embraced the cross and endured challenges with faith and courage, teach us to persevere in times of trial. Help us to trust in God's providence and to find strength in His grace. Pray for us, O holy St. Bridget, and accompany us in our own crosses and struggles. Amen.

Day 9:

O St. Bridget, who now enjoys the eternal bliss of heaven, intercede for us before the throne of God. Obtain for us the graces we need, and help us to follow your example of love, virtue, and devotion. Pray for us, O holy St. Bridget, and lead us closer to God both in this life and in the life to come. Amen.

May the intercession of St. Bridget of Sweden bring us closer to God, inspire us in our journey of faith, and guide us in living lives of holiness and virtue. Amen.

Conclusion

In conclusion, St. Bridget of Sweden's life and teachings have left an indelible mark on the religious, social, and cultural landscape. Her deep spirituality, commitment to social justice, and dedication to reform have inspired countless individuals throughout the centuries. From her mystical experiences and encounters with divine figures to her writings and interactions with political and religious leaders, St. Bridget's impact has transcended time and continues to resonate with people today.

Her devotion to God, devotion to Christ, and emphasis on personal prayer and contemplation have provided spiritual nourishment to those seeking a deeper connection with the divine. Her calls for moral reform, care for the marginalized, and promotion of social justice serve as a reminder of the ongoing need to address injustices in society and promote the dignity of all people.

The establishment of the Bridgettine Order and the dissemination of her writings have further solidified her influence, providing a framework for religious life and a source of spiritual guidance. The continued veneration of St. Bridget through pilgrimages, feast day celebrations, and devotion demonstrates the enduring impact she has had on the faithful.

St. Bridget's canonization by the Catholic Church and the recognition of her holiness reinforce her status as a saint and exemplar of Christian virtue. Her legacy lives on through the devotion of those who seek her intercession, study her writings, and draw inspiration from her life.

St. Bridget of Sweden's life and teachings stand as a testament to the power of faith, the pursuit of righteousness, and the transformative potential of one individual's commitment to God. Her enduring impact serves as a reminder that, through a life dedicated to God and the pursuit of justice, it is possible to effect positive change and leave a lasting legacy of love and compassion.

St. Bridget's relevance in the modern world

St. Bridget of Sweden remains relevant in the modern world, as her life and teachings offer timeless lessons and inspiration. Here are some ways in which St. Bridget's relevance persists today:

1. Spiritual Guidance: In an increasingly busy and secular world, St. Bridget's emphasis on personal prayer, contemplation, and devotion to God provides a valuable reminder of the importance of nurturing one's spiritual life. Her teachings encourage individuals to seek a deeper relationship with the divine, find solace in prayer, and prioritize spiritual growth amidst the demands of daily life.

2. Social Justice and Advocacy: St. Bridget's commitment to social justice and her advocacy for the marginalized remain pertinent in today's society. Her teachings challenge us to address systemic injustices, fight against discrimination, and care for the vulnerable. St. Bridget's example inspires individuals to be agents of change and advocates for a more just and equitable world.

3. Moral and Ethical Conduct: St. Bridget's emphasis on moral integrity, honesty, and ethical behavior serves as a guiding principle for navigating contemporary challenges. Her teachings remind us of the importance of living with integrity, upholding Christian values, and treating others with compassion and respect in our personal and professional lives.

4. Empowerment of Women: St. Bridget's example as a strong and influential woman in a patriarchal society continues to inspire and empower women today. Her advocacy for women's rights and her leadership within the Bridgettine Order challenge gender biases and serve as a reminder of the valuable contributions that women make in all aspects of life.

5. Balance of Contemplation and Action: St. Bridget's ability to integrate contemplative prayer with active service provides a relevant model for individuals seeking a balanced approach to life. Her teachings encourage us to cultivate a deep interior life while also actively engaging in acts of charity

and service to others. This balance reminds us of the importance of both personal spirituality and outward expressions of love and compassion.

6. Cross-Cultural and Interfaith Dialogue: St. Bridget's international connections and encounters with diverse religious and political leaders demonstrate the importance of cross-cultural and interfaith dialogue. Her example inspires individuals to engage in respectful and meaningful conversations, promoting understanding and cooperation among people of different backgrounds and beliefs.

7. Inspiration for Personal Transformation: St. Bridget's personal transformation and spiritual journey serve as an inspiration for individuals seeking personal growth and transformation. Her story encourages us to embrace the possibility of change, to pursue holiness, and to strive for a deeper and more authentic relationship with God.

In summary, St. Bridget of Sweden's relevance in the modern world lies in her timeless teachings on spirituality, social justice, moral conduct, empowerment of women, and the integration of contemplation and action. Her life serves as a beacon of inspiration, challenging us to embrace our faith, work for justice, and strive for personal and societal transformation in our contemporary context.

Lessons to be learned from her life and example

The life and example of St. Bridget of Sweden offer valuable lessons that can be applied to our own lives. Here are some key lessons we can learn from her:

. Deepen our Spiritual Life: St. Bridget's unwavering devotion to God and her commitment to prayer and contemplation remind us of the importance of nurturing our spiritual lives. We can learn from her example by making time for prayer, reflection, and seeking a deeper relationship with the divine.

. Pursue Holiness and Virtue: St. Bridget's pursuit of holiness and her embodiment of virtues such as humility, compassion, and integrity inspire us to strive for moral excellence. Her example encourages us to grow in virtue, develop a strong moral compass, and seek to live a life pleasing to God.

. Advocate for Justice: St. Bridget's commitment to social justice and her advocacy for the marginalized teach us the importance of standing up for what is right. Her example reminds us to use our voices and actions to challenge injustice, promote equality, and strive for a more just and compassionate society.

4. Embrace Personal Transformation: St. Bridget's own journey of personal transformation demonstrates the possibility of growth, change, and spiritual renewal. Her example invites us to examine our own lives, identify areas for growth, and embrace the process of transformation towards becoming the best versions of ourselves.

5. Foster Dialogue and Understanding: St. Bridget's interactions with individuals from diverse backgrounds highlight the importance of dialogue and understanding. We can learn from her example by engaging in respectful conversations, seeking common ground, and promoting understanding among people of different beliefs, cultures, and perspectives.

6. Empower and Support Others: St. Bridget's leadership and support of women, as well as her compassion towards the poor and marginalized, teach us the value of empowering and supporting others. Her example encourages us to uplift those around us, advocate for the rights and dignity of all, and use our resources to make a positive impact in the lives of others.

7. Live a Life of Service: St. Bridget's life of service, both through her acts of charity and her dedication to the Bridgettine Order, reminds us of the importance of selflessness and serving others. Her example challenges us to use our gifts and talents to benefit others, whether through volunteer work, acts of kindness, or contributing to the well-being of our communities.

By reflecting on and applying these lessons from St. Bridget's life and example, we can strive to live more purposeful, compassionate, and spiritually enriching lives.

Glossary: Key terms and concepts related to St. Bridget and her story

Here are some key terms and concepts related to St. Bridget of Sweden and her story:

1. Mysticism: The belief in or experience of a direct, personal, and unmediated union with God or the divine. St. Bridget's mystical experiences and revelations played a significant role in her spiritual journey.

2. Visions and Revelations: St. Bridget reported receiving divine visions and revelations throughout her life. These were supernatural experiences in which she claimed to have direct communication with God, Jesus Christ, and other holy figures.

3. Devotion: St. Bridget's profound devotion to God and her unwavering commitment to a life of prayer, contemplation, and service. Her devotion served as the foundation of her spiritual life and inspired others to deepen their own faith.

4. Reform: St. Bridget was an advocate for reform within the Church and society. She called for moral renewal, justice, and integrity in religious and political leadership, emphasizing the need for a more authentic and heartfelt expression of faith.

5. Bridgettine Order: The religious order founded by St. Bridget, officially known as the Order of the Most Holy Savior (Ordo Sanctissimi Salvatoris). The Bridgettine Order follows the Rule of St. Augustine and focuses on prayer, contemplation, and acts of charity.

6. Canonization: The process by which an individual is officially recognized as a saint by the Catholic Church. St. Bridget was canonized in 1391 by Pope Boniface IX, affirming her sanctity and elevating her to the status of a saint.

7. Intercession: The act of asking a saint or holy person to pray on behalf of oneself or others. St. Bridget is venerated as a powerful intercessor, and believers often seek her intercession for various intentions and needs.

8. Feast Day: A specific day designated to honor and commemorate a particular saint. St. Bridget's feast day is celebrated on July 23rd, the anniversary of her death, in the liturgical calendar of the Catholic Church.

9. Contemplative Prayer: A form of prayer focused on silent reflection, stillness, and seeking union with God. St. Bridget's emphasis on contemplative prayer reflects her belief in the importance of silent communion with the divine.

10. Social Justice: The pursuit of fairness, equality, and the promotion of the well-being of all individuals in society. St. Bridget's advocacy for social justice highlighted the need to address systemic injustices, care for the poor and marginalized, and promote a more equitable society.

11. Revelations of St. Bridget: A collection of writings that document St. Bridget's mystical experiences, dialogues with Christ, and spiritual insights. These revelations were compiled into a book known as the "Revelations of St. Bridget," which has had a significant influence on Christian spirituality.

12. Dialogue with Christ: St. Bridget's mystical encounters often involved direct conversations with Jesus Christ. These dialogues were characterized by deep spiritual teachings, guidance, and personal messages from Christ to St. Bridget.

13. Pilgrimage: St. Bridget undertook several pilgrimages during her lifetime, visiting sacred sites and holy places associated with the life of Christ and the saints. Pilgrimage was seen as a means of spiritual growth, penance, and seeking divine blessings.

14. Spiritual Director/Confessor: St. Bridget had a spiritual director and confessor named Master Matthias, who played a crucial role in her spiritual

ourney. He provided guidance, interpreted her visions, and supported her
n her reform efforts.

5. Popes: St. Bridget had interactions with several popes of her time,
ncluding Pope Urban V and Pope Gregory XI. These encounters involved
liscussions on matters of faith, sharing her spiritual experiences, and
eeking papal support for her religious endeavors.

6. Apostolate: St. Bridget engaged in an apostolate, which refers to the
ctive sharing of the Gospel and the promotion of the faith. Her apostolate
nvolved advocating for reform, teaching, and guiding others in their
piritual lives.

7. Discernment: St. Bridget's spiritual journey required discernment, the
rocess of seeking and understanding God's will for her life. Discernment
nvolved prayerful reflection, seeking guidance, and making decisions in
lignment with God's plan.

8. Relics: St. Bridget's relics, which are physical remains or objects
ssociated with her, are venerated by the faithful. Relics serve as tangible
onnections to the saint and are believed to possess spiritual power and the
bility to intercede for the faithful.

19. Legacy: St. Bridget's legacy refers to the lasting impact of her life, teachings, and example on individuals, communities, and the Church. Her legacy includes the continued devotion and veneration of her, the influence of her writings, and the ongoing inspiration drawn from her holiness.

These additional terms and concepts further enrich our understanding of St. Bridget's story, spirituality, and influence, offering insights into the various aspects of her life and the broader context in which she lived.

MAY THE LORD BE WITH YOU!

THE END

Made in the USA
Las Vegas, NV
10 November 2023

80584187R00049